Love, Life And Light

Murmurings of the Mind

Preetika

BookLeaf
Publishing

India | USA | UK

Dedication

Naina and Hachi
My eternal blessings

Preface

It's strange how thoughts visit at odd times like when I am
in half dream state; when I am giving a belly rub to my
elder one or running after the younger one to get her ready
for school; when I am super tired and suddenly there's a
spark; or when I am drying clothes outside and looking
back to see if my daughter has finished her milk or not.

These poems are reflections of people and things around
me, what I perceive and how I have lived through
different stages of life. Written over the years and some
more recently, they all have one binding glue - love. Hope
you feel it.

Acknowledgements

I am forever grateful to God for guiding me and showing me light. Thank you Life for your experiences, bitter and sweet, inspiring me to write. Thank you to the publishing team for stitching together everything wonderfully.

Friendship

When the night is young and
People are curling in bed
I meet you for a ride
To the moon and back

We walk and talk, eat and smile
Your bag of stories always full
Some half-chewed, some digested
Most of them out of experience recounted

On a bench here or there
On flight of steps or feet
We place our conversations bitter or sweet

Licking chocolate off our spoons
Laughing and drinking the last drop
The clock sends occasional reminders
But we don't listen, we won't stop

The warmth of a friend

The gentleness of a gentleman
The laughter of an amused man
You have it all, you lay it bare

You flout the norms and show you don't care
May you live long
forever young and strong

Abandoned Love

I Love You
I wish I could say these words to you
When we were little and could have met
Under the shade of the mango tree
Eating chocolate, licking it off each other's hands
Chasing each other in the scorching sun

I Love You
I wish I could say these words to you
When we were teenagers hardly knowing each other
Without holding the fingers, I would have let you know
While playing in the ground or accompanying our
mothers to the market
How it felt to be near you

I Love You
I wish I could say these words to you
When we grew up a little more
When the doors to the imagination opened
And our minds slowly succumbed to the softness in our

hearts
I would have let you know
How much I wanted to look at you

I Love You
I wish I could say these words to you now
A hundred times and more
When our paths have diverged
And distance has grown manifold

I Love You
I wish I can say these words to you long after
Our bodies have become wrinkled and haggard
But the heart burns with passion
Longing to hold each other in life or death

You and I

On a moonless sky
Without a star twinkling near the corner of my eye
Cold wind gently stroking my hair
No search, no grief
Everything is still and placid as my soul tonight

Why don't you come and play in my arms
Why do you not stop being beautiful despite your flaws
We can 'feel' the swing or run down the stairs
Chasing each other's dreams, building a secret
camaraderie

I will not disturb you in your hours of sorrow and
reflections
It is the only thread that binds me to you
But come tonight my dear
To engulf me in your light and create the warmth inside

Love Hurts

Some nights seem longer
Some paths never end
Some pictures never fade
Some smiles never tire
Some hands never paint
Yet knit a beautiful story

Some mistakes are repeated
Some lessons forgotten
Some friends are missed
Some mates stay together
Some days are tough
Some hours are too light

Some years melt into fleeting moments
Some deep-seated desires are met
Some unsaid wishes come true
Some words are unspoken, understood
Some stories are untold, woven

Some hearts give tender love and care
Some eyes, they simply dance.

Dusk to Dawn

I search for thee on a dark winter night
Tired but hopeful that I will find you
As the wind kisses my cheek, I re-visit the lanes you
never walked with me
Sitting in the balcony I move ahead in time, without you
Smiles fade away sadness slips in
Tears gush down heavily
"Take it easy", someone said
The phone rings and it's You
My heart leaps up to the sound of your voice
From a casual hello to the usual laughs
Everything comes to a standstill
As the call ends the pulse stops racing
The unsaid goes unexpressed
Silence is yet again taken for granted
Nevertheless, I settle for it
The night gets colder and darker
Numbness covers the wounds
I search for thee
Until the dawn.

Celebrating Life

The cocktails were ready
Tables were set right
Marigold in yellow and orange
pinned on the chairs looked so bright

Dancing people, holding hands, winking and
Swaying in each other's arms
Basket lights dropped from the ceiling here and there
The *dhols* continued to play in a rhythmic trance

Fragrant petals in red
Adorned the path waiting for its stars to shine
Fireworks one after the other
Illuminated the night sky

They walked hand in hand
Radiant in blue and white
Celebrating love in its splendour
Taking blessings as the newly weds

The Wish

Like the morning dew upon the cold palm
Like the effervescent laugh on the lips of a three-year old
Like the silence between the naked lovers sitting by the
window
Like the cluster of stars hovering over the crowded head
Like the eyes that glisten with hunger and
shamelessness,
Like the madness of a vagabond walking towards the
unknown
Like the windy night removing the peels of sorrow,
slowly
Like You and I, torn and apart, forming a coherent whole
Like the wish itself, born in the mind, nursed in the heart
and never told
Like love, surpassing the boundaries of the known,
traversing the limitless possibilities with that one wish

Daddy

Lift me up daddy
To touch the stars and bring home some
In my birthday party tonight
Where the moon will brighten all corners
and make faces sparkle in the night
Where *Mowgli* and *Bagheera* will stand tall on the cake
And flowers will adorn my crown, sitting upright

Lift me up daddy
To pick delicious mangoes and taste some lychees
Lying untouched in the cane basket
To share your burden
As you shop my favourite jams and pickles
And help mamma prepare meals I love

Lift me up daddy
To make me strong and confident
As I face the realities of the world and
Overcome weaknesses of my mind
To guide me when I am low

To console me when I cry
To love me always, and make me and mamma shine

The Light

Far away there lives a loner
Moving towards the light at the end of the tunnel
When the world outside lit up by sunshine and hope
Is buzzing with activity, making merry
Ah, what a sight!
The loner is walking treading the path
Lit up by the flames of her heart
Defeating time, battling against history
Making soft, slow movements towards the future
Defined by her memory
Undeterred by broken lines of destiny
With a look so gleeful
Glistening eyes and a carefree smile
Every movement guided by her will
And made stronger by the 'only wish'
She profoundly believes in
Carelessly moving in a trance
Music of life reverberating through her senses
intoxicated by love
A whole new world within

Delicate on the fringes, a sponge inside
She is moving towards her 'light'
The light at the end of the tunnel
She keeps moving
But the fire has extinguished.

Beginning

I desire no more, it eludes me
I speak no more, words don't come easily
I write no more, lost my imagination
I hear no more, I am dumb
I look no more, only stare
I shout no more with a parched heart
I doubt no more, the truth has defeated me
I end here... a new beginning awaits me there

The Woman

I will woo you with a smile and drive you crazy
I will arouse your curiosity and silence it with a wink
I will chase you when you go away and then never let
you go
I will walk with you till the end of the road and beyond
I will give you my hand but not my trust so casually
I will look in your eye and melt your heart
I will caress you like a feather and hold you with passion
I will dance with you in the rain and wipe away your
sweat
I will love you to the core, with my deepest emotion

I am the wind to swipe away your sorrows
I am the bare land where you can sleep in peace
I am the river to quench your thirst
I am the sky to let you soar high

I am a Woman, the Woman you dream of, the one you
have.

Homecoming (in Haridwar)

A home I never lived in
But always feels I breathe inside every day
It's whitewashed walls and vast courtyard
Where guava, mango and lychee trees stand tall
Makes me reminiscent of a past I never spent there

A home that echoes the bond of friendship and love
Where cuckoo sings and peacock dances
Where hide and seek is a ritual and
'Who eats food first?' is an everyday game

A home where man's best friend lives carefree and is
loved deeply
Where voices speak in harmony
Where mornings arrive holding a cup of tea
And evenings are chirpy in front of the tv

A home that resonates with common beliefs and joy
Where colours and crackers create their magic, kites fly
high

Where neighbours are family and guests are friends
Where time is a storyteller, each day is lived with fun

Hachi

That pair of eyes
Glistening with love so pure
Swelled up with pride on waking up
Eagerly wanting to go back to sleep again
Deep and expressive, large and innocent
Never winking, full of mischief

He looks at me to say something
Do I understand?
Oh, yes! Time for him to go for a ride
Flapping his ears jumping over the rough patches
Marching ahead in style

Whimsical in nature
Playful in behaviour
He runs after people he doesn't like
My darling Hachi is one-of-its-kind

He licks off the vanilla so swiftly
Doesn't leave behind a trace for us to find and wipe

Wagging his tails on hearing his name
Napping morn to noon all the time

Balloons

Pink, green, yellow and mauve
Round and fat, big and small
Hung on the roof or
Floating in the air
Some look like rabbits
Some fly like aeroplanes

A child looks eagerly upwards
Clutching her mom's hands tightly
Smiling as she glances towards the red one
Making excuses to grab one

At times alone, sometimes hanging around in a bunch
Looking pretty and colourful every moment
Whether in a party or at home
Playing with balloons is super fun

Solace

I want to break free
From the pangs of my wounded heart
That pins me to your love and betrayal
Leaving me alone in long hours of silence in the dark

I want to break free
From memories of passionate nights
From jealousy and heart burns
Mindless wanderings and madness I cannot hold

I want to break free
From unspoken words, unwanted arguments, losing
direction
From the fear of having conversations
To save our hearts from the ruins

I want to wake up
To hear the voice of my soul
Telling me to pause and reflect

To silence the chaos of the mind and
Walk in the direction of happiness my heart now attracts

The Dress

I didn't know what I was looking for
Until my friend saw right there
As usual I was driven towards the black
But it was grey this time as my state of mind right now

Sleek, curvaceous, elegant
Standing together facing the mirror
We were in awe of each other
She looked stunning and I felt beautiful.

I turned around watching everyone
Clapping and cheering for the two of us
Made my way to the desk thanking everyone
To pay for my first dress as I was turning 31

How Silence Looks

Silent eyes
Hidden truths
Unveiled tremors
Unending battles
Unfulfilled dreams
Tasks accomplished
Heavy sighs
Shadows of delight
Expectant mornings
Darkness personified
Unexpressed pains
Joys manifold
Lost possessions
Growing distances
Moments melting away

Shimmers of delight
Uninvited premonitions
Unwanted solutions
Ruthless desires in secured arms

Visions of hope

in hackneyed phrases

Estranged bodies

Relations re-defined

Questions unanswered

The gateway to search within

Broken mirror inside out

Promises unmade

Vows unbroken

Voices in the turbulent sea

Floating on its surface quietly

Ripples of memories

Subsiding, rising gently

Old lanes re-visited

Unknown roads traversed

Footprints left, erased

A still gaze...

Such is Life

Life's a lesson to learn
Seeds of happiness to grow, gloom to burn
No matter what the path
Keep walking without looking back

Days of sorrow may not end
Nights might seem harder to spend
Do not stop, do not delay
Where there is faith, there cannot be any doubt

Look inside your heart and be strong
There's nothing that can go wrong
No matter what the outcome
Do not give up your dreams for anyone

Fuel your goals with passion
Give wings to your perceptions
Build courage, be kind and stay strong
Bad days are not going to stay for long

Hope

A four-letter word with enough power
To attract positivity in the need of the hour
In bad times or good
It can uplift you as it should

Nothing is permanent in this world you see
One's loss is someone else's gain as you see
If you lose out on an opportunity
Hope is all you really need

Friend or partner, brother or sister
It drives relationships and circumstances
When the lights go down and there's darkness around
Hope is the elixir to keep you alive you will see

www.ingramcontent.com/pod-product-compliance
Lightning Source LLC
LaVergne TN
LVHW010951200726
843509LV00013B/2367